From Rags to Riches

Table of Content

Introduction

"From Rags to Riches: Mastering the Art of Making Money"

In a world where financial success seems like an unattainable dream to many, there is a burning desire within us to break free from the shackles of financial restraints and transform our lives. We covet the opportunity to push the boundaries of the current situation, rewrite the narrative from penniless to rich, and master the art of making money.

This book is a guiding light that illuminates the path from the depths of adversity to the heights of wealth. It is a compass that gives us the strategies, mindsets and practical wisdom we need to build a prosperous future. "From rags to riches:
Mastering the art of making money is an invitation to a transformational journey, a journey that goes beyond just making

money and embraces personal growth, fulfillment, and realization of our true potential. Within the pages of this book we embark on a journey of exploration and self-discovery. We clarify the common misconceptions that accompany the path from poverty to wealth and break down the illusions that hold back our progress. We delve deep into the power of thought and understand that our thoughts and beliefs are the keys to unlocking the door of abundance.

With each turn, you'll learn practical techniques for moving from a scarcity mindset to an abundance mindset. We learn to organize our thoughts, cultivate gratitude, and embrace the endless possibilities that exist in the realm of wealth creation. We discover the resilience and determination needed to overcome the obstacles that inevitably appear on our path to wealth.

The following chapters will explore the intricacies of financial literacy, identifying lucrative opportunities, and developing multiple revenue streams. We learn the art of negotiating and selling to leverage technology and the digital economy to sustain success while giving back to society.

But this book is more than just a compilation of strategies and tactics. It is an emotional journey that unlocks the depths of our desires and longings. It urges us to face our fears, challenge our beliefs, and unleash our power. It lights a fire within us and reminds us that we can achieve great things and change lives.

As you embark on this transformational quest, be guided by the understanding that the journey from rags to riches means more than just material wealth. It is about striving for personal growth, realizing our dreams and realizing our true potential. It's about creating an abundant life, not just for yourself, but for those around you. So join us on this extraordinary expedition. A journey that uncovers the art of pushing boundaries, exceeding expectations and making money. Solve mysteries, face challenges, and unlock hidden treasures together. Embark on a journey of self-discovery and transformation as you master the art of making money and shape your destiny from rags to millionaires.

Chapter 1: Unmasking the Rags-to-Riches Myth

In our quest for wealth, our minds often wander to compelling stories of people rising from the depths of poverty to the glory of wealth. Painted with nuances of hope and inspiration, these stories ignite a fire within us and inspire us to believe that such transformation is within our own reach. But as we embark on this journey, it's important to shed layers of illusion and debunk the penniless-to-rich myth.

We are often tempted by the allure of overnight success stories. You'll see headlines about people whose lives changed in an instant, with a stroke of luck or a game-changing idea. We are drawn to these tales like moths to a flame, waiting for a chance meeting with destiny. But behind these stories lie hidden truths and unexplained struggles.

The reality is that the path from poverty to wealth rarely rises quickly. It's a difficult climb filled with obstacles, setbacks, and moments of despair. We know that true financial success requires unwavering dedication, relentless hard work, and resilience that outweighs any fleeting moment of good fortune. Debunking these myths and controlling our expectations is critical. Overnight success is the anomaly, the exception, not the norm. The media may highlight extraordinary stories, but they do not reflect the reality faced by the vast majority of people who want their economic situation to improve. Success, true and lasting success, is built on a solid foundation of realistic expectations and long-term strategy.

Setting realistic expectations requires understanding that the road to prosperity is a marathon, not a sprint. It takes patience, perseverance and the willingness to weather the storms along the way. There will be times when progress seems stagnant, when setbacks feel insurmountable, and when questions arise. But it is moments like these that test our resolve, and our resolve must remain unyielding.

A long-term strategy is your compass for navigating the unpredictable realm of wealth creation. It requires careful planning, informed decision-making, and continuous learning. It's not enough to expect good luck or rely on instincts. We must educate ourselves, acquire the necessary skills, and remain adaptable in the face of a rapidly changing world. Success requires a proactive approach, a willingness to embrace change, and a commitment to personal growth.

To debunk the rags-to-riches myth, we need to confront our own illusions and redefine our understanding of what mastering the art of making money really means. It's a journey beyond fairy tales into the world of hard work, resilience and strategic thinking. By recognizing the challenges, defying myths, and embracing reality, we can gain the clarity and determination we need to embark on this transformational journey.

Chapter 2: Cultivating a Wealth Mindset

In a world where financial success is often viewed as the ultimate measure of wealth, cultivating a property mindset is an important aspect of achieving true wealth. The path to nurturing the spirit of the wealthy goes beyond mere money-making strategies. It is a shift in our thoughts, beliefs and attitudes towards wealth. This article delves into the importance of cultivating a prosperity spirit and explores practical steps to embrace wealth and pave the way to financial freedom.

Change your mindset:
Cultivating abundance begins with fundamentally changing your beliefs about money and abundance. It requires letting go of limiting beliefs that keep you from pursuing financial success. We do not view money as a scarce resource, but believe that

there are abundant opportunities and resources at our disposal. This mindset shift lays the foundation for prosperity and abundance in our lives.

Accept positive affirmations.

Positive affirmations are powerful tools for rewiring our subconscious mind and strengthening our belief in financial abundance. By repeating positive statements about wealth, success and prosperity over and over again, we reprogram our thought patterns. Affirmations such as "I deserve to enjoy abundance," "Money flows into me effortlessly," and "I attract opportunities for financial success" redefine the way we think. , helps us align our thoughts with the reality we want to create. Seeking knowledge and education:

In order to cultivate a wealthy spirit, it is important to acquire knowledge about finance and acquire culture. Reading books, attending seminars, and following renowned financial experts can provide valuable insight into wealth building strategies and investment opportunities. Improving your financial literacy will enable you to make informed decisions and take calculated risks to achieve your financial goals.

Adopt a growth mindset.

To develop a prosperity mindset, a growth mindset is essential. See challenges as opportunities for growth and learn from failures as stepping stones to success. A growth mindset enables you to persevere in the face of obstacles, adapt to changing circumstances, and continuously develop your skills and knowledge. By making setbacks temporary and maintaining a positive outlook, we develop resilience and the ability to bounce back stronger.

Surround yourself with like-minded people.

The companies we run have a huge impact on how we think and act. Surrounding yourself with wealthy-minded people who share similar financial goals can provide you with inspiration, support, and valuable insight. Joining networking groups, attending financial seminars, and seeking guidance from successful people all help create a positive environment that nurtures our high net worth mindsets and encourages us to aspire to greater financial success. help.

To activate:
The mindset of the wealthy is not enough. Achieving financial prosperity requires action. Developing a high net worth ethos involves taking calculated risks, seizing opportunities and implementing sound financial strategies. You need to set clear financial goals, develop an action plan, and consistently take action to reach those goals. Aligning thoughts with purposeful actions

closes the gap between thoughts and tangible results.

Chapter 3: The Foundation of Financial Literacy

Emotions flicker within us like a flame as the chapter that holds the key to our financial liberation, the foundation of financial literacy, begins. It's a journey of curiosity, excitement, and perhaps a little anxiety. We are standing on the edge of knowledge, ready to unravel the mysteries and get the tools to help you navigate the complexities of personal finance.

The foundation of financial literacy is not just a collection of facts and figures. It is a transformative awakening that empowers us to make informed decisions, build resilience and lay the foundation for a prosperous future. It begins with a commitment to learning, a willingness to delve into the complexities of money management and capitalize on growth potential. Central to this foundation are the key concepts of budgeting, saving and investing, the pillars that form the foundation of our financial journey. Budgeting is the art of wise allocation, the conscious act of tracking income and expenses and aligning financial resources with goals and values. It is the means by which we manage our finances, curb wasteful spending, and pave the way for the accumulation of wealth.

Saving money is also very important in the pursuit of financial freedom. It embodies the power of delayed gratification, the conscious decision to save money for the future. By saving, we can weather the storm, seize the opportunity, and build a safety net that brings peace of mind. Developing the habit of saving sows the seeds of stability and lays the foundation for growth.

Investments with growth and wealth creation potential tempt us to expand our horizons. It is the strategic use of our financial resources to travel the world of assets, manage risk and increase yields. Investing requires understanding a variety of investment tools, staying informed, and making calculated decisions that align with your financial goals. It's a dance between risk and reward, an initiative that offers the potential for financial independence.

As part of financial literacy, we also discuss the practical aspects of debt management and credit building. Debt can be a powerful growth tool if managed wisely, but it requires attention and understanding. By understanding concepts such as interest rates, repayment strategies, and debt management techniques, you can protect yourself from the pitfalls of excessive debt and build a balanced financial life. At the same time, building trust gives you access to opportunities and secures your financial future. This includes understanding your credit score, establishing a good credit history, and adopting responsible lending practices.

As we traverse this world of financial literacy, we experience a mix of emotions: the excitement of newfound knowledge, the empowerment of being in control of our financial destiny, and the relief of overcoming the complexity that once overwhelmed us. To do. Through continuous learning and a commitment to personal growth, we have the tools to make informed financial decisions, build a strong foundation, and pave the way to lasting prosperity. Is included.

In this chapter, we embark on a journey of education and self-discovery. Delve into the intricacies of budgeting, saving, investing, debt management and credit building with practical tips and insights. We open our hearts to accept all concepts, break old beliefs and unlock the true potential of economic life.

As we move through the realm of financial literacy, we need to appreciate the emotions associated with this change. Let your curiosity drive your quest for knowledge, your enthusiasm will drive your desire for growth, and your determination will empower you to seize the opportunities that lie before you. Together, we lay the foundation to grow our financial dreams and bring us even closer together.

Chapter 4: Identifying Lucrative Opportunities

In the vast expanse of the ever-evolving business landscape lies an area of opportunity - a world of many opportunities to take advantage of those with the vision that identifies them. Emotions swirl within us – a mix of shades of anticipation, curiosity and entrepreneurship – in this chapter we aim to unravel the mystery of identifying and capitalizing on these profitable ventures. I was.

Recognizing market trends and emerging industries is a compass that guides us to untapped potential. It's the ability to observe changing consumer preferences, technological advances, and social change. As we immerse ourselves in the world of business, our senses sharpen, our eyes sweep the horizon, and our hearts beat with excitement at the prospect of being at the forefront of innovation. Conducting thorough market research and analysis makes it a reliable ally for gaining insight and unveiling hidden gems. We dig deep into the intricacies of our chosen fields and leave no stone unturned. Our goal is to understand customer needs, competitive landscape and industry dynamics. Market research allows you to make informed decisions and uncover gaps waiting to be filled and niches that crave change.

Strategies for identifying and capitalizing on profitable opportunities are shaped in sharpening our instincts and sharpening our entrepreneurial acumen. We cultivate a mindset of curiosity, always seeking new knowledge, and keeping abreast of industry trends. We advocate calculated risk-taking and recognize that the big gains are often beyond your comfort zone. We encourage creativity, encourage the mind to wander, and explore unconventional paths that can lead to unprecedented success.

But this chapter is not just about strategy and tactics. It is a journey that ignites our emotions and touches our soul. It's about using our innate intuition and having the courage to dream big. It's about fostering a sense of purpose, aligning our passions with market needs, and pursuing ventures that interest us.

Emotions are heightened when you imagine possibilities and dreams that come true. There is tension in the air, and an obvious energy that propels us forward. It is the thrill of the hunt, the thrill of discovering opportunities that can change our lives and the lives of others. It's the feeling of empowerment that comes from recognizing your potential to create something great. Embrace the emotions that come with this journey as you delve into the world identifying lucrative opportunities. Let your passions drive change and pave the way for success. Use your intuition, trust your instincts and venture into uncharted territory. Embrace chance and recognize that the most special occasions can come unexpectedly.

In this chapter, we embark on an exciting journey that combines analysis, creativity and intuition. We have the tools to spot market trends, conduct in-depth research, and strategize for success. But most of all, we embrace our emotions. The fire within us that fuels our quest for excellence, our unwavering belief that we have the power to identify and seize lucrative opportunities.

Enjoy the emotions that accompany this journey as you navigate this realm of possibility. In hopes of discovering the next big thing, we propel you forward, let the thrill of possibility course through our veins, and the joy of creation light our way. Together we open the gates to a world of untapped potential.

Chapter 5: Developing Multiple Streams of Income

The realm of financial abundance holds profound concepts that awaken our entrepreneurial spirit, which is the key to unlocking our true earning potential. It's about the idea of creating multiple streams of income that are a web of passion, ingenuity, and a burning desire for financial freedom.

As we begin this chapter, a mixture of excitement, determination, and liberation wells up within us. We are at a crossroads and ready to explore opportunities beyond traditional employment. We aspire to leverage our skills, talents and assets to create a harmony of income streams that brings us closer to our financial goals in harmony. Exploring different sources of income beyond traditional employment ignites an insatiable curiosity within us to challenge the status quo and seek alternative paths to financial success. We believe our skills extend far beyond the limits of a single job or career. We dare to dream, pave our own path, and use our unique talents to generate income in ways that match our passions.

Leveraging our skills, talents and assets will be our way of doing things and will drive us to diversify our income streams. We discover hidden talents, improve skills and unlock creative potential. We seize opportunities to monetize our expertise, whether it's freelance work, consulting, or turning a hobby into a profitable business. We recognize the value of our unique abilities and refuse to confine them to the realm of mere entertainment.

Diversifying our income streams is central to our quest to improve financial stability. We recognize the dangers of relying on a single source of income and being vulnerable to economic fluctuations and unforeseen events. By generating multiple streams of revenue, we weave a safety net that softens turbulent times. We explore opportunities such as investments, royalties, passive income streams, and even starting our own businesses, all of which contribute to our mosaic of financial well-being.

Emotions run high as you begin your journey of generating multiple revenue streams. There is a feeling of liberation from the chains of limited income potential. Envisioning a life of financial independence and the freedom to pursue your passions sends excitement through your veins. Determination drives our actions and keeps us going in the face of challenges. We are driven by a vision of a life in which financial prosperity is not just a distant dream, but a tangible reality.

In this chapter, we embark on a journey of exploration and empowerment. We identify income opportunities, leverage our unique talents, and learn how to diversify our income streams. We represent an entrepreneurial mindset that seeks to adapt, innovate and seize the opportunities around us.

Embrace the emotions that come with this transformational journey as you navigate the realm of developing multiple streams of income. Enjoy the exhilaration that comes from pursuing your passion while generating income. Celebrate the freedom that comes from being freed from his single paycheck. Stand tall, united in the belief that our earning potential knows no bounds.

Together, we approach this chapter with unwavering determination and an open heart. We boldly dream big, defy imposed restrictions, and create financially prosperous lives through the harmonization of multiple income streams.

Chapter 6: Mastering the Art of Negotiation and Sales

Emotional Intelligence:

Central to mastering negotiation and selling is emotional intelligence, the ability to understand and manage one's emotions and empathize with others. Emotional intelligence enables individuals to connect with customers, understand their needs, and create solutions that resonate on a deeper level. By attuned to the feelings of both parties, negotiators and sellers can create a win-win situation that fosters long-term relationships.

Build relationships:

Building good relationships is the cornerstone of successful negotiations and sales. The aim is to create trust, understanding and connection with the other person. Emotions play an important role in building relationships because they allow people to form genuine connections based on shared experiences, empathy, and a shared sense of purpose. By actively listening, empathizing, and adjusting your communication style to match the other person's emotions, negotiators and salespeople can build strong relationships and lay the foundation for success.

The power of storytelling:

Stories have a huge impact on human emotions and can be a powerful tool in negotiations and sales. By crafting compelling narratives that reflect audience emotions and desires, negotiators and sellers can elicit influential responses and influence the decision-making process. Stories create an emotional connection, making information more memorable and engaging. It enables negotiators and salespeople to effectively frame their messages by tapping into their desires, fears, and hopes.

Overcome Objections:

Opposition is inevitable in the world of negotiations and sales. But good negotiators and salespeople don't see objections as obstacles, but rather as opportunities to address underlying feelings and concerns. By actively listening to opposing views and taking the other person's point of view, individuals can uncover root causes of resistance and offer personalized solutions to alleviate concerns and build trust. Emotionally smart negotiators and salespeople turn objections into stepping stones to success. Creating Win-Win Solutions:

The ultimate goal of negotiations and sales is to produce a win-win solution that both parties are satisfied with and feel is of value. Emotions play an important role in achieving this result. By understanding the emotional motivations and needs of others, individuals can develop solutions that not only meet their own goals, but are deeply aligned with the wants and aspirations of others. The ability to deal with and appeal to emotions enables negotiators and sellers to reach mutually beneficial agreements that foster long-term partnerships.

Resilience and Confidence:

Mastering the art of negotiation and sales requires resilience and confidence. Emotionally intelligent people understand that not every negotiation or sales pitch leads to immediate success. However, they remain confident in their abilities, learn from their setbacks, and persevere in their pursuit of positive results. Effectively managing their emotions helps negotiators and salespeople stay calm, adapt to unexpected challenges, and exude confidence that inspires trust in their customers and counterparts.

Chapter 7: Leveraging Technology and the Digital Economy

Use of technology and the digital economy: Enabling Exciting Transformational Journeys

In our fast-paced world, technology is the engine of progress and change. From how we communicate and access information to transforming entire industries, the digital revolution has opened up a world of opportunity and created an emotional roller coaster. Individuals and businesses are taking advantage of this wave of innovation and harnessing its power. They embark on an exciting journey that harnesses technology and the digital economy alike.

There is excitement in the air as we witness rapid advances in technology. The advent of smartphones, cloud computing, artificial intelligence, and the Internet of Things has opened the door to a realm where connectivity knows no bounds. With one touch, we can navigate vast amounts of information, reach out to people around the world, and access a seemingly endless selection of products and services. The world has truly become a global village, and the anticipation of what lies ahead evokes a sense of euphoria.

In the digital age, the economy is undergoing a major transformation. Traditional industries are being turned upside down and new industries are emerging due to the endless possibilities of the digital environment. E-commerce has revolutionized the way we shop, giving us the pleasure of browsing online and having it delivered to our doorstep. The gig economy allows individuals to explore their passions and talents, creating a sense of freedom and empowerment. Startups and entrepreneurs are driven by the prospect of turning ideas into reality, and the thrill of innovation drives them on that journey.

In addition, technology democratizes access to knowledge and education, creating opportunities once unimaginable. Online platforms offer courses, tutorials, and learning materials to anyone with an internet connection. This entitlement evokes a range of emotions. The hope that individuals will acquire new skills and improve their employability. A commitment to personal growth and success. I am so grateful that the digital world is bringing education to the most remote corners of the world. Still, this exciting journey is not without challenges and emotions. Rapid technological change requires continuous adaptation and lifelong learning. Fear of being left behind can be overwhelming, but with the right attitude and thirst for knowledge, individuals can overcome these fears and embrace the exciting opportunities that lie ahead. As the industry evolves and changes, the digital economy needs resilience and agility. The thrill of innovation drives us, but the fear of uncertainty can be daunting. But with perseverance and a willingness to take risks, individuals and businesses can navigate the twists and turns of this digital roller coaster and emerge stronger from it.

On this exciting journey, it's important to use technology responsibly. Cybersecurity and privacy concerns play a large role, reminding us of the need to balance innovation and protection. As we navigate our digital environment, a sense of vigilance and vigilance arises to ensure that our personal information is protected and our online experience is safe.

In summary, embracing technology and the digital economy is an emotional and exciting adventure. From a passion for innovation and enhanced knowledge, to the fear of uncertainty and determination to overcome challenges, this journey captures the essence of human resilience and adaptability. By embracing technology with an open mind and spirit and harnessing its power responsibly, we will master this digital roller coaster ride and create a better future for ourselves and generations to come. Ready and ready to be reborn.

Chapter 8: Sustaining Success and Giving Back

In the Twilight of Victory, immersed in the brilliance of our achievements, we come to a crossroads. It is the intersection of sustained success and social contribution. A mixture of gratitude, responsibility, and the desire to leave a lasting legacy runs through our veins. In this chapter, we embark on a journey beyond personal wealth, exploring strategies for maintaining financial stability, safeguarding wealth for future generations, and harnessing the transformative power of philanthropy. increase.

Wealth preservation and long-term financial stability are our compass and guide us through the ever-changing tides of the financial landscape. We recognize that success is an enduring journey, not an instant. We employ prudent financial practices and adhere to the principles of budgeting, prudent investment and diversification. We maintain an asset preservation mindset and understand that sound financial decisions today are the foundation for a secure future. We value financial literacy, continuously improve our knowledge, and adapt to changing economic conditions. With each step, we strengthen the pillars of financial stability to ensure continued success beyond the present.

Strategies for preserving wealth and transferring wealth across generations reveal the importance of heritage that extends far beyond our lives. We recognize a great responsibility to safeguard our wealth for future generations—a responsibility that goes beyond mere material accumulation. We utilize estate planning strategies such as trusts and endowments to protect our wealth and ensure a smooth transition to the next generation. We foster financial literacy in families and instill the wisdom and values that underpin sustainable prosperity. We teach the importance of good stewardship and foster a legacy that goes beyond mere wealth.

The importance of philanthropy and giving back requires us to embrace our role as agents of positive change. We recognize that true wealth is not only measured by financial success, but also by the impact it has on the lives of others. We believe in the transformative power of giving that broadens our horizons, enriches our lives and strengthens our sense of purpose. We are committed to philanthropy whether we donate money, donate time or expertise, or use our influence to drive social change. We recognize that giving back can have far-reaching effects far beyond our own, strengthening our communities and creating a more just world.

A range of emotions will intertwine as you embark on a journey of sustaining success and giving back. As we look back on the journey that has brought us here, we are filled with gratitude. Responsibility rests on our shoulders, reminding us of our duty to protect our wealth and share it wisely. When we recognize that we can make a transformative impact on the lives of others, a deep sense of purpose develops within us.

In this chapter, we embark on a transformational journey that transcends personal gain and embraces a broader vision of prosperity. We discover strategies to maintain financial stability, maintain prosperity for future generations, and weave the web of philanthropy into the fabric of our lives. Embrace the emotions that accompany this extraordinary journey as you move through the realms of lasting success and giving back. Let gratitude be the driving force behind your actions and remind yourself of the abundance you have received. Make responsible decisions and ensure your assets serve a purpose beyond your personal needs. Let us be driven by a deep-seated sense of purpose to create a more compassionate, fairer world.

Conclusion

In the tapestry of life, we explores the intricate threads that connect rags and riches. Within the pages of this book, we dive into the realm of possibility with knowledge, determination, and a burning desire for financial success. We explore myths, develop a wealth mindset, build a foundation of financial literacy, identify lucrative opportunities, create multiple revenue streams, master the art of negotiation and sales, and leverage technology and the digital economy. and learned the importance of sustained success. and give back.

An emotion emerged within us that was a symphony of hope, excitement, determination, and a thirst for growth. We have embraced challenges, overcome uncertainty, and overcome obstacles. In this transformational journey, we learned that true wealth is more than the accumulation of material possessions; I discovered that

Since the rags-to-riches myth was debunked, we've shattered illusions and embraced the reality that success is the result of long-term strategy, realistic expectations, and unwavering commitment. We've seen the power of mindset and how it can have a huge impact on how we do business. By cultivating resilience, determination, and a rich mindset, we have overcome setbacks and thrived in the face of adversity.

Fundamentals of Financial Literacy guide us, providing us with the tools and knowledge to navigate the complex world of personal finance. We have embraced the concepts of budgeting, savings, investments and debt management and harnessed their power to build a solid financial future. Armed with this knowledge, we set out to exploit emerging trends and market dynamics to find profitable opportunities.

We are broadening our horizons and looking for diverse sources of income beyond traditional employment. By leveraging our skills, talents and assets, we have discovered new ways to create wealth, diversified our income streams and improved our financial stability.

Negotiation and sales skills are your ally in finding favorable results. We've honed our communication skills, delved into the psychology of persuasion, and built fruitful relationships. With each negotiation, we have closed lucrative deals, promoted cooperation and expanded our reach.

The digital sector has leveraged the power of technology and the digital economy to drive economic success. Through e-commerce, social media and online marketing, we have navigated the connected world, seized opportunities and expanded our reach to a global audience.

But our journey does not end with personal gain. We know how important it is to be successful in the long term and give something back. We have a responsibility to protect wealth and foster a legacy that goes beyond mere wealth for future generations. Through our philanthropy and donations, we have embraced our role as agents of positive change, transforming lives and creating ripple effects that have a lasting impact on society.

At the end of this book, let's carry on the insights we've gained, the emotions we've felt, and the unwavering determination to move our journey forward. Remember, true wealth is measured not only by your financial success, but also by your impact on the lives of others. Continue to grow, evolve and take advantage of the opportunities that lie ahead.

Move forward with courage, wisdom and compassion. May you find fulfillment not only in your personal success, but also in your ability to encourage others.

www.ingramcontent.com/pod-product-compliance
Lightning Source LLC
Chambersburg PA
CBHW070859220526
45466CB00005B/2049